The Night of Stones

THE NIGHT OF STONES

POEMS BY

George MacBeth

Macmillan

LONDON · MELBOURNE · TORONTO

1 9 6 8

© George MacBeth 1968

Published by
MACMILLAN AND CO LTD
Little Essex Street London WC2
and also at Bombay Calcutta and Madras
Macmillan South Africa (Publishers) Pty Ltd
Johannesburg
The Macmillan Company of Australia Pty Ltd Melbourne
The Macmillan Company of Canada Ltd Toronto

PRINTED IN GREAT BRITAIN BY
THE BOWERING PRESS PLYMOUTH

attar of roses in the night of stones

ACKNOWLEDGEMENTS

Some of these poems have appeared in the following magazines: *Catholic Education Today, The Listener, The London Magazine, The New Hungarian Quarterly, The New Statesman, New Worlds, The Poetry Review, The Spectator,* and *The Twentieth Century.* To the editors concerned my acknowledgements are due.

CONTENTS

I

DRIVING WEST

I

No, there was nothing first. Only his air
Stretching for ever, as it seemed. And wind
Cool on their dying faces from the hills
Where cars moved through dark forests, bearing gifts
And laughing children to the caves and mines
Far to the West. Where there was pine-scent, wheels
Hung in that air, turning each corner, stilled
On the brink of something.
                     What was clear to see
Lay under lenses, burning in their dream
As they flew in. Bathed in such draughts of blue
As crowned his eyes, in clarity of means,
Awkward for nothing, they began the end
In even patience. And all followed, swift
As had been promised.
                  Then, the summer lake
The war-lord wrote beside, his buttoned coat
Up to his neck, his long eyes evenly
Disposed, flung back the sun.
                    To clapping hands
Each furled his flowered wings. And flowing rain
Came as before, and went, and washed them clean
Of all that blood-fall.

II

            Shielding his thin heart
He drove West as the day died : and the sun
Blazed in his face, clear dazzling like a brass
Cauldron to see the past in, or a gong
Booming with echoes.

3

Life was thick with cars
Moving to meet the sea. That summer men
Spent the long draught of gold in going home
To what they loved, the shore. So when it came,
Darkness with all its visors down, it hurt
More than they knew. At first it seemed too bright
For anything but wonder.

Low in the sky
The first blow was the blow of light : that night
Its crescent flowered in the East. It cut
Through glass of cars, through heavy walls of stone,
Through skull and fruit. And men like monks in cells,
Bowed on their knees, hands clasped behind their heads,
From zinc-lined solitude were shaken clear
And bathed in darkness. Miles of open light
Swallowed the naked and the lame. From this
No one walked through, and saw.

The second blow,
After such radiance, was the blow of heat
As if an oven opened, or as if
An oven closed.

The third blow was the blow
Of blackened wind. No frame of concrete stood
Near to the storm-boss unsplit. Blackened wind
Solid as iron was the mate of flame
And cooled the beaten anvils.

When it closed,
Then there was calm. Calm, and the ash. And while
The city rose towards red sky in the East,
Far Westwards like an earthquake in the heart
It felt. Flung forwards by the blast, his head
Broke on the screen. Skin parted, and the blood
Moved in the shape of lightning.

Touched, with eyes
To see with, scarred, he saw. His clothes were stuck
To his back with sweat. Wet, shaking, he lay still,
Racing his head. Then one by one he moved
Ear, nose, lip, jaw, neck, waist, groin, knee, wrist, toe.
He was alive. He rose, then, pressing fists
Into what moved.

4

Miles down the road, past shreds
Of metal with their meat gone, gouged or stayed,
He saw the cans. Pumps fallen, petrol-smell
And air gushing from a gashed tube. *Here, then,*
He thought, *I can live here.* Heaped cans of oil
Shone below stars beside him.
                              So he turned
And fell head foremost to the gushing air
As the sun rose. And while it climbed in blue
He slept, marked with his blood.
                                And as he dreamed
Under the draught of air, his mind flowed out
And far down to the wells of darkness. Once
A short man with an axe beside a stream
Butchered a calf, and in the dream its heart
Fell on the grass, and crawled. Another time
Around a castle men who moved like pines
Grew to a noose that strangled. Old, asleep,
Washing slow hands in water, she was there,
Grey-haired and guilty, waiting for their thumbs
To choke her blood and stone.
                              Then he woke up,
Screaming : and, waking, head askew on cans
Of spilled oil, counting minutes, hearing wind
Sigh in the sunlight, knew that withering stone
Had caused her first death.

III

                    He drove back through blood,
Thinking of her. And as he drove things changed :
Noon-light to evening, there was nothing left,
Only a world of scrap. Dark metal bruised,
Flung soup of blood, anchors and driven screws :
The whole dead sea of wrecks lining the road
Emptied his mind. Ship after painted ship
Thrown into crumbs. He drove through nothing, dazed,
Awake, and dreaming.

5

                    Burning to the East
Where the city burst and scattered its fine seeds
Into the lap of air, the fires had died.
Only the veins, the main straight roads bored in,
Bordered by drifts of dust. Life thinned from stone
Through grit to powdered ash.
                              So he drove on,
Knowing his quest was meaningless and blank,
Towards what might have been. Then, by a curve
Where the road narrowed, as it should have done,
He parked the car, got out, and went on foot
To where she might have died.
                              There was no sign
Of even iron or fireclay. Stooping down,
He reached out his right hand to brush the dust
And part some, delicately, where she used
To part his hair. As if in sand he stroked
The shape of something in the dust, some shape,
And touched his eyes.
                       Then he stood up, and took
A new coin from his pocket. With his heel
He dug a flat hole, flung it in, and scraped
The ash back over it, speaking aloud,
Or meaning to, these words : *Where we lived first,*
Below our window, when they changed the house,
Workmen found coins. They proved its date, showed
   pride
Of earlier workmen for their blood-fall. Here
I show the same, where there is nothing. Only
The ceremony remains.
                         And then he drove
Out of the dust-bowl, and across the plain
Back towards his refuge, and his cans of oil,
All that the war had brought him and forgot,
Or tried to for a little, what had died,
Having done all he could.

IV

                  Then, as before
That spear-flash in the evening, most were sick
And needed blood, knowing they all were doomed
As she was.
                  Awake under buckled steel,
After what lapse of hours she stirred and moved
Still in the tunnel. There was no more light,
No train movement. Somewhere a faucet dripped
Water, blood, water on stone. Inside her brain
The blood beat back.
                  Fire was the sign of blood.
After the first blow it returned and beat
Over and over at those broken doors.
It oozed from coal-trucks in a rush of blue-
gold, yellow as gas here, mustard-sharp.
They smelt it coming. Acrid hint of smoke
Under carriage-cloth. Rake of hot-iron heat
Flaring on cheeks. And then that fast-back lick
Of its long tongue, flickering through each crack
In plastered skin and bone, liquid like knives
Cutting and salting. Wincing in its wounds
The whole train split like stitches.
                  Men fought with tins
For knives to open tins. Bone-wounds from strikes
In the long club-war of survival healed
And left them hobbling. Over all that fire
Waiting to burst its banks and bleed them dry
They crouched like hens.
                  There leather creased and wore
Around low shoulders that were scarred with hawks
From earlier wars. Where in the wall men burned
For being nothing, thunder and leaves were borne
With songs of triumph. Wrenched from these, and oiled,
In coats of black too seared with flame to cool,
Some walked and ruled. Walked when the last cars
    broke
And there was no more fire. In wars for this,
And pride, over the brick-waste they patrolled,

7

Circling like rooks. And when they found, they killed :
Or cured what insolence was left, ingrained
From scoured-out power, in pain.
                          Stumbling on rails
Towards that ring of sun, past sweating walls,
Or in her mind, as he had done, she moved
To that church, where she was due.

V

                          There by the grave
Beside slow falling clay she stood in dirt
And watched their heavy faces. Brass and lead
Had stamped their moulds in blue eyes and in brown
Before it happened. Under bells that speared
The cold larks in the clouds, the feuding clans
Blackened the day with grieving.
                          Far away
She saw the cows come downhill to cold farms
And feed on warm hay. Breathless, she recalled
A tight sow with her farrow in her skin
Scraping a nest of sticks for him to fall
And come alive in.
                          Waxed clay into clay,
The passage was performed. The oiled ropes ran
Under and over. And bronzed lion-masks
Amazed the worms.
                          Men coughed and stamped And bones
Long bearing stress of birth were spared and fell
Into the space below the world they penned
Her glassy eyes in.
                          In earth, in wood and stone,
The coffin-shape lay where it rested. One
Bowed in his hands, tears falling. Hard as ice
He was a winter cave where water flowed
Through aeons of slow time. The other stood
Seeing the keels beach in a sea-weed blaze
Along the Western shore-line.

8

                                    Layer on layer
The dwindling pyramid of the dead bled in
Over their faces. Red with heat of kin
After the cold earth, by the common grave,
They saw it coming.
                             Beyond her wrecked train
Outside that warring town she felt the chill
Take hold of her.
                        That history of men
Marching with axes over these bared fields
Heraldic now at mid-day, mailed her brain
In heavy chains.
                        She sniffed, and felt hard rot
Smeared like an ointment, strangely thick and sour
Against her skin, ash-breath of coming death
Among the old. Old as they all were old
And he would soon be.

VI

                        Up the mourning stairs
All the white dogs turned round their eyes and frowned
As he came on. The cases creaked and stirred
With what was in them. Silence of clear glass
Behind which all the world could hold its breath
Until the moment came to scream, shivered
And knew its hour.
                        Holding that corpse in mind
The hall was taut with waiting.
                                    Then blood broke
Over each surface it had oiled before
In even violence. Absolving red,
Crackling with iron spikes, it struck and spilled,
Swilling jet-metal. Cold wood shook and peeled
Under such pressures that the whole house bulged
Like a bag of water. Willy-nilly, walls oozed
Thick drops, then, blotched with patches, bleached

        9

One even red. What was a refuge once
Wilted to a grave.
                        That night for the first time
Under one roof, sheltering from their grief
With port and ham, the cousins met. Like a dog
Blood ran between them with its nose to the ground
Sniffing for a scent. One slapped his covered sides
With a brace of gloves like a killed pheasant. One
Hunched his dead side, slurring his vowels like
A load of stone. What there was left to say
Under that flood of grieving no one knew
Except through money. Making, moved by, coins :
This was their only link. Hands shook that shook
Each other's hands. One with his stomach-wound
From alcohol, one rigid from the stroke
Of what had struck him as a child. Each merged
With the sores of Nature.
                        Outside, through blood, the kilns
Burned in the distance, and the bricks were fired,
Squared moulds for men, each holed with a dish. Men
   stoked
The rain-slaked furnaces with coke. Men scarred
Ledgers with ink. These were the fields of war
Where lines of men, black figures, marched and fell
Into the red of death. Hungry or old,
Some lay beneath bricked urns they built and sold
Miles from the houses they put up and bought
All beside slag, soot sifting down through clouds
Of massed rain.
                        And that night the Eastern ash
Gathered and swayed them to the gulf of war
Where all were game-soup. So the cousins met
Behind the kilns, under that night of blood,
Dying, and proud. And no-one spoke, or knew
How they could speak.
                        Her father sat alive,
Dreaming of horses. It could come again,
Come once, and still his guts, they said, would hold
For a year and a day. If he could smoke and play

The bricks could scatter. There were colours, odds
Of another win. So he lay back in tweeds
Beside her cairn, drinking his wine. *Here, then,*
Here's something for you, here, he said.
                                    Then blood
Broke in her dream, as dams break in the brain
To flood the cells. She dreamed of men and guns,
Keys jangling in a tiled hall, and a race
For broken glass. And then it all began
To merge in dazzling anguish of hot lights
Gashing the dark, gushing on walls.
                              Coughing,
Tossing on red sheets, weeping in her dream,
She knew the end was near. She touched her hair
And felt grey rain turn into hail, white snow,
And cried for him.

VII

              And as he drove he heard,
And stopped the car, and came to where she was,
Far in, still in the tunnel, blocked, alive
Behind her shattered glass. Her locked hands moved
Like brooched snakes round a cup. There cold red wine
Swirled like his blood. Her burned legs spread, she
    looked
Ready for death. He kissed her, touched her arms
Gashed to the wrists with red. Her knitted scars
Wove them a skin.
                    Far East the city fell
Into itself. Welded in white heat, fused
Under that hanging sword, they grew as one,
Her cold pearl coming to his shell-bred hands
In milk and scent of musk.
                          That second night,
Sleeping with her, he dreamed his father came
And frowned above him. Wearing black and mud,

11

He drew high pillars. Coal burned in his eyes
And beams collapsing choked him. Wind and sea
Broke through the hall they talked in, till they drowned
In flowers. Clematis, dark spider, touched
His cold face with her seven hands. He smiled
In his own garden once again. She moved,
His mother, shearing blooms. He was a child,
Married and dying in his mother's arms
Far from the war.
            And then at noon he woke
With her dead in his arms. She who had lived
Yards from the blast, though miles beyond the blaze,
Dazed with the air had sickened. And so he
Lifted her up, and held her in his hands,
Her black hair falling.
            Then his walk began
Back to the light-ring and the drifting ash
That would drown him soon, too. Toiling on rails,
Cracked up, he reached the pocked air. Hard and thin
His new breath came. He turned. And as the sun
Sank in the sky, he felt the poison stir
And knew the end was near. Starting his car
He drove on West, the ash-light in his eyes
Glazing the skin with gold. As in his grave,
Wearing his death-mask, he moved into dark
Behind the wheel.
            And as he drove he seemed
To wake and dream. Two knights lifted their swords,
One with a hawk on his left hand. His feet
Sloughed the rough dust as though on skis in snow
Near to his mountains in the East. Across
That blazing sea, beside his level bay
From which the coarse earth rises, the long port
Waited for his return.
            And the other came
Short-necked and dark-haired, who had burned his
    palm
With a slow match. And looking to the light
Above the chair he lay in, stared and slept,

Though waking, to resist the pain. These two
Moved in his dream as he drove on and felt
The poison stirring.
                          So the sun went down
And the car moved on into the Western dark
Nearer and nearer to the sea. Those cans
Of lost oil lay behind, missed long ago
Like her, and their slow burial of the blood,
In gathering black. He heard no horn, no drum,
Only the waves breaking towards the shore
His headlamps bored at. And the gentle ash,
Feather of pity, settled in the wind,
Swirling to fill the earth.
                          So he drove on,
Wading in blood. And, as before and since,
The crown was lifted, and he sank to sleep
In darkness.

VIII

                          And so driving in his dream
He reached the last beach. And the waves washed in
Over the waste sand where no others were
Except his past. There with his wooden spade
And coloured pail he walked along the wall
Searching for where to build. And where the sea
Came to its highest mark below the road
He made her mausoleum.
                          The war of coins
Boiled to a cream of spume. Here all that blood
He bathed and came from soaked his grains with salt
And filled the shifting turrets.
                          Far away
Furled in their fresh cocoons the butterflies
That broke the city slept. And bowls of tea
Passing from hand to hand confirmed the signs
Moving in open pages, quaint and fine.
Their line continued. Pictures in the wind
Sailed into water.

13

And on Western sand
Where he was dying the sharp water leapt
And seethed over the moat, sinking away,
As his dark royal blood sank, through all time.

IN THE NORTH

I   The Sacrifice

    Whole trees fell in the night,
Half-burned.
    Outside the hut, beside the lake,
One willow dipped its white fur in the water,
Hissing.
    Walking on cones, through spruce, she felt
The first touch, brushing her ankle.
          Close to the headland
She saw the heaped logs. Trunks of birch, unstripped,
Still wet from water, in their open frames
Drawn down for this from higher up, lay stiff
In roped stacks.
    All one night, in air
Of lilac near the lake she lay awake,
And dreamed. She saw the black, brown-headed swallow
Building its nest of earth below the eaves
Hack at a shell ; and when it broke, a snake
With forked tongue spat through.
        Chewing roasted flesh
Spiked over metal, she could taste the raw
Red blood of elk.
    Slowly the year burned on
Towards its mid-point. Where she walked, half-bared
From steam or water, weeds blazed.
        Every noon,
Thrashed red with silver birch, she cooled soft flesh
In water.
    Gaping vetch along the bank
Reached in its velvet lips towards her.
         Black
With rust the stove-pipe worked clear.
       She lay prone,
Watching the nights burn. All that blackened air,

15

Flame-scarred, sank into brightness. She was scored
With inward burning.
                              Singed along the skin
By nettles, she rolled over, crushing flies,
Closing herself. Through nests of ants she felt
Each hour grow ripe.
                              Under the drone of bees
Her world grew in. The closed leaves wrapped their
     claws
And gripped the whole wood. Owls flew low and
     passed,
Knowing no prey.
                              Alone she aged in flame
Along the blood, feeling the heart pulse out
Through June. In dying fire, she burned.
                                        And when,
Exactly at the mid-year, dressed in flame,
They carried her in column through the pines
And stripped her breast, parting her naked legs
Before the sun, her clenched purse broke, and
     spent
Its catch of seeds high on the white trunks.
                                        Red
At midnight to the red sun her pyre blazed.

II   *A Revel*

                    That night the sun burned late.
Long after it had sunk below the lake
The fire-dance raged.
                    Girls dressed in blinding frocks
With ribbons in their drenched hair whirled and
     screamed,
Flowered with scent.
                    Gnats rose. And in the heat
Of flaring resin, labouring men bit off,
Spitting, the stems of grapes.

16

                        That sultry night
Girls were in flame. Their blackened locks glowed red,
Grated in coal. Astride the pine floor, fired
With foaming beer, their close doors opened. All
Danced for a siege.
                        Men were their partners in
One urgent salient : they thought in pairs,
Axed in each other's arms.
                        One danced alone
Whirling in separate fire. Slow, as she moved,
The white moon followed her, bathing her hair
In light.
            Settling in tune, she drew it down,
And moving, as the whole room paused and watched,
It danced around her.
                        In a sluice of gold
It poured below her shoulders, flushed and swayed
In lazy light.
            Amidst that plot of crows,
Ice-white it shone.
                        Men touched her, one by one,
Twisting her body like a pole, to flag
And furl it in.
            Half-laughing, she spun off
Along her own line, salmon-smooth. So cool
From ice below the poise of others, she
Moved sleek and clean through waters of each waltz,
Tensed for herself.
                        That hair like sea-weed swung
In flowing essence of hot scent. It eased
And fired.
            So many felt it silk
In tensions of their dreams, they turned, half-struck
With plans.
            Uncoiling, scaled like silver, she
Soothed like a waterfall of melting snow
Their long desire, then swayed in sickening flame
Up the rough bark of bodies mailed with need
Whose eyes were paired shears.

                17

                    Hacked off, combed, unwound
In tangles on the blood-silk straw of barns,
Her hair became her. It was what she was.
Ash-willow in the wind, it whirled and soared
As if alive.
            Then, for a simple jest,
One lifted it as it was whirling, pulled,
And brought it burning from her barren crown
And showed her naked.
                    Panting, she stood still,
Stripped of her light.
                    Then, turning, like the moon
Sinking in silver through the blackened weeds
In one clear swoop, she scarred the lake with blood.

The dance was over.

THE MOON-BIRD

*What she wanted was to live. Live as the great
moon bird did that she had seen over these pale,
pure, blue skies, with its mighty wings outstretched in the calm grey weather; which came
none knew whence, and which went none knew
whither; which poised silent and stirless against
the clouds; then called with a sweet wild love-
note to its mate, and waited for him as he sailed
in from the misty shadows where the sea lay; and
with him rose yet higher and higher in the air; and
passed westward, cleaving the fields of light,
and so vanished; — queen of the wind, a
daughter of the sun; a creature of freedom, of
victory, of tireless movement, and of boundless
space, a thing of heaven and of liberty.*

Each night it came. In that locked house, her brain,
It was dark early. Solid curtains hung
Blocking the windows to the sea. The sun
Set into fish. None saw it. Her long eyes
Turned inward to the print of blazing towers
In awkward rhyme.
                And then each night that bird,
When it grew dark, at about ten o' clock,
Circling above the strained nerves of her room
On quiet wings, outlined against the clouds,
Hovered, and waited. She could feel its wings
Revolving, stroke air. And she heard the boom
As waves broke, raking shingle on the shore,
Withdrawing, exhausted.
                If it heard its mate
In the distance, it would scream : one long high cry
Breaking across the darkness. From the mists
Out in the sea, he answered. Low and clear
As bells to ships in trouble, struggling up,
He called, called, called.

                    Then he would come,
Darker than darkness. Quiet now, his call
Dropped in her windows like the first warm rain
Fresh from the West. There both of them were bound,
Redoubled by the beat of wings. And to their rock
Far out at sea, against the rising sun
In the morning, she could feel their flight begin,
The tug of oars.
                    Then, as their heaving wings
Drew the dark air together, pushed it back,
And parted slower as they broke and pulled
Like long ships faster for the unseen shore
She felt her cold life quicken.
                              In her dream
Stretched out in glory on a wall of gold
Her cold legs arched and scissored, and she moved
Like someone swimming in God's holy fire
Until, through sweat and silvered flame, she came
As they did to that lonely rock, far out
Across the breaking waves.
                              Then she awoke.
Rising, she drew the curtains. It was day.
The sun-bird walked in silence on the sea.

AN EGYPTIAN SEQUENCE

I   *The Jar*

Before the screen, above the fan and fire,
   The owl-god listens. In his head
The dark scent beckons to her moving hair
Far off in Egypt. Here, faint odours curl
Where all her cataract of blossom fled
      Through broken air
   And lost rich essence to the mire
In open sands. I feel the stars unfurl

Their coat of attar in her ease of mien
   And foreign silk. Across the rain
In images of fibre she withstands
All touch of grease. It is her hair that turns
The purple of my night to blood again
      With moving hands,
   Living, for all to see. Her screen
Opens beyond the owl-god. Incense burns

Behind the secrets in the jar of time
   Before she lived. Such depths of coal
Blaze out of lacquer in his lonely beak
That breaks in gold ! I hear lost music sigh
Through the bare hall. And now, as though the whole
      Core of the bleak
   Refrain of brilliance in the rime
Under the sands of Karnak flowers, I

Shiver in water, shed my skin and see
   Her grow and live again. I bow
Under the owl-jar, lift his head and smell
Her oiled hair falling, hear the flowers and fruit
Blooming in bowls. It is the moment now.
      I taste the bell
   Ringing in darkness. And her bodies flee
Into a lion pawing at my foot.

II   *The Lioness*

She leaps out of the stars. In gorgeous black
   I see her moving in a mine
Where coal is blazing in her eyes with green
    And forests walk
Sowing the East. I feel her pale leaves track
The scent of honey. Over all my wine
Still pregnant with the grape I taste the sheen
Of Karnak moons. I follow her and talk

Through light and rubies of the larks men kill
   For holy sport. Her dark eyes burn
Over the tunnels where the trees have died
    Into the floor
Weeping their dew. Her long robes arc and spill
Where we are drinking. Far away men turn,
White hunters, and I see their cold mounts hide
Faces of night. And she is here in store

For daughters of the sun to live and die
   In wonder at her skin. I raise
Onto my shoulder the pale badge of tin
    Whose open scar
Absolves our parting. Faltering, I try
To reach through eddying smoke and touch the glaze
Blue on her arms. I know her brittle skin
Melts through my hands. And all that bodies are

Before the filament of dross be fired
   Sears to a thread. I feel her shrink
In muscle to those walls where all began
    Aeons before
Our burning fingers touched. O, I desired
That lioness for mine. Now if I think
She was the one I lie. I am the man,
But she is locked in gold beyond the door.

He builds her house. It lifts a holy spire
Out of the morning, and the gates of ice
Crack into clear gold. Somewhere out of sight
    A white flare wanes in Karnak. Spice
From all the islands gilds her. In slow fire

The night dissolves. I watch her in fresh light
Walk to its windows where the folded leaves
Drip with the sap of plenty. Girls with rings
    Tinkling beneath their heavy sleeves
Gather hot feathers from the crest of night

And set her brow. Her arms are lifted springs
Rich with the tempo of delirious cold
In running silk. I hear it hiss and flow
    Out of her shoulders, poured and rolled
Essence of glad wings. Over her she flings

A shoal of attar, and her peacocks glow
To greet the day. It is her house she owns
In all her splendour of disruptive brown
    Breaking the spectrum. Child of bones
Yielded from foreign cedar, she bows low

Before the dawn sun, dips her hand in down
And seals her lips. *I love my house,* she breathes
In secret to his cooled heat. *Here am I,*
    Thy servant, in a world that seethes
And waits thy blaze, naked beneath my gown

In moving light. And while she stoops, the sky
Clears into ever brighter depths of blue
Stripping the night. The sun steps through her house
    And warms the stone. And she is true
To her one room where all the ages lie.

THE DEATH-BELL

I see you enter through the silver door
    Under the tail. To where your throne
Rests in its grooves, you move on naked feet,
Alive, and well. Strapped in, you sit alone.
I see your toes, white worms along the floor,
    Carved as in glass. Our cold eyes meet,

Mine across miles of waiting, as before.
    No, in some lethal under-tone
I sense one difference. You slide your seat
More gently, with your polished knuckle-bone
White on its arm. I hear a strange wind roar
    As you take off, brilliant and neat,

Into the air. I think I feel it more
    Than when it happened. In the drone
Of all that wind, air gathers to repeat
My sense of why. Once it was like a stone
Locked riding in the heart, as in a store,
    And soon to grow, and bloom, like wheat

Beside the sea. My blood-thing, in the core
    Of our green love I heard you moan
Like oceans on the shore, driven by sleet
Against my neck for safety. All I own
Sinks into this : that we are still at war
    And burn like soldiers in the heat.

The sun dies into space. Your bright wings bore
    Holes in the blue. As in a cone
Through which salt drifts and falls, even and fleet,
Your body drifts through silence. Lightly blown
By air from tubes above your head, one spore
    Of what we called love drops, dead meat.

PRAYER TO THE WHITE LADY

after Himnusz Minden Idoben
by Laszlo Nagy

I

Creature of flame, out of
the sun's bow I call you :
moment of crystal for the throwing-knife,
    lighten my darkness, I
need you now.

II

O, lady of the small larks,
keeper of the instruments
in the zenith, last room of the king,
    lighten my darkness, I
need you now.

III

Palm in the rain of sorrow,
fire under glaze, lifting
the twin domes of your body above me,
    lighten my darkness, I
need you now.

IV

Mistress of Victory, flame
of the gathering storm, brightening
into the jails of my eyes,
    lighten my darkness, I
need you now.

27

V

Nurse of the war-wounded, yours is
the house of the Jew and the Negro :
draught of the bee's kiss, mysterious honey,
   lighten my darkness, I
need you now.

VI

Lady, oblivious of blood and money,
belly-dancer of hunger, echo
and resonance of the millennium,
   lighten my darkness, I
need you now.

VII

O, my dear one, tempered
by the beam of the laser, torn
by the stone body of the gorgon, the man-child,
   lighten my darkness, I
need you now.

VIII

Always your tall house was open to me,
glittering with expectation : O, godlike
above the bronze cauldron of your beauty,
   lighten my darkness, I
need you now.

IX

In the beginning I felt your body lap me,
drowning into the saraband of love :
killer of the black crows that haunt me,
   lighten my darkness, I
need you now.

X

Now, on the brink of the vacuum, at the edge
where the million tendrils of nothingness
are erupting, even out of my own mind,
     lighten my darkness, I
need you now.

XI

Lady of pain, sharer of this affliction,
sufferer under the same electric coil :
now, as I reach for the dark pill and the needle,
     lighten my darkness, I
need you now.

XII

Only in you will the house of my body glisten
gold in all its chimneys and veins :
only in you will the white pigeons flicker,
     lighten my darkness, I
need you now.

LIVING IN THE ECHO

I *The Dark Skin*

> I see two women, walking
> into the darkness away
> from me. One
> is the one I am losing
>
> now, the other
> the one who was lost
> in the darkness and
> came out.
>
> There is no end, only
> the women walking
> slowly with bowed
> heads into the
>
> darkness, the light
> behind, always
> behind, and my
> own shadow
>
> breaking
> over their bodies, the
> dark skin
> against the light.

II *The Ocean*

> Similarly, another
> came. She was in
> the jealous ocean
> of where
>
> that first
> was wanted
> still. Or had
> been once.

30

Only to the door
of where there
had been
other moments, it

lasted, though.
Leaving something, seeing
the salt
burn

through its eyes. O
so slowly the
draining
starts, the draining.

III   *The Invisible Present*

So many of them. Funnelling
out of the
clear high circle
ahead

of me, into
the invisible present, out
and down,
past the outstretched

hands, over
the dam,
wearing away the
rocks. These are the

loved ones, the
cataract of
their pressures, blinding
my eyes.

31

IV   *The Heirs*

> Watching something, with
> rinsed tin all round
> us, a low jet
> ironing silence
>
> out. It
> must have been soon
> then, the
> crash. Or
>
> perhaps in
> the holes between
> that possibility, something
> settled. We
>
> are the heirs
> of it, one
> turning into
> two.

V   *At The Time*

> *O, if it were
> so,* the
> bitter think, feeling
> the sharp edges
>
> gripping
> closer to their own
> soft eatable
> marrow. *O,*
>
> *if it were
> so, the flints
> arrowed
> back, brittle but*

serviceable,
on the vicious
loved hands. Not
that it could

be. No.
That is,
when it hurts,
matters, I

mean, at the time.

VI   *The Globe*

I saw your country
like a heart
bleeding
into the sea. So many

worms there,
under their
burning glass, crawling
in green, to

make one
yard of
silk. And the grinding
eyes

of the last eagle, shot
from a truck. My
worm, my eagle, your
eyes bleed, soiling

the globe.

33

Living in the echo
of all that
resonance, I
complain

sometimes, even
now. Was
it so far over
the hot

stone to
fold hearing
in, listening
for the dust

out of the
crevices, feeling
its way
back to

a new
whole ? No, it
was only how
the raw

mind saw it, fooling
with other
commitments, wanting
a pillar of salt.

A RIDDLE
for Ponge

I

It is always handled
with a certain

caution. After all,
it is present

on so many private
occasions. It goes

into all our darkest
corners. It accepts

a continual
diminution of itself

in the act
of moving, receiving

only a touch
in return. If a girl

lays it along
her cheek, it eases

the conscience. It salves
the raw wound,

nipping it clean. To be
so mobile

and miss nothing
it has to be

soft. It is.

II

Consider
the pornography

of its
nightly progress. It moves

between our legs
like a ghost

lover, melting
into essence before

those
elaborate organs. As

underwater
flowers, they close

against it. So
many

resistances, such
rich

anticipations!

III

It is like
ourselves, malleable,

strange-smelling,
subject to the hands

of women in
so many postures. We

38

take it to our skin
in thin

layers of itself,
our image. It

loves water
as we do. In that

the bean-stalk
riots

as lovingly
as a dolphin. In

that
it lives, easing

its whole
body, unto

death, slowly.

THE SOFT WORLD SEQUENCE

I *The Sea*

Through the glass floor,
from below,
he could see the girl
in the glass typing-chair,

in the glass skirt,
crossing her flesh legs
over the glass eye
in her groin. Glassily, it stared

at his own eye, and slowly,
the world of glass,
opening, closing,
became soft,

like the lips of an octopus
with eight legs
opening, closing,
in the Arctic ocean.

II *The Clouds*

The man had been a bit
slow on the uptake, but
when his elbows went through
the light oak,

he saw the point. After his leg, too,
had sunk in
and was shivering
in the middle of the carbon-paper drawer, they began

to realise just how far
it had gone. Not even
the one in the telephone
bothered about the screaming then,

though it did make a hell
of a noise. It was how
to profit from it that occupied
all their minds. After so long

without anyone wondering
how they felt about it all,
none of them was accustomed
to making much of an impact. So

even the one in the floor
let him run his legs through
for a while without
worrying. Of course,

the man did wade in diminishing
circles, evidently
grasping (albeit rather slowly)
just how soft the whole

thing had become. It took him
several minutes, though,
to appreciate the full reason
for the watery coolness.

When he did,
there was more noise. The one in the PAX phone
got quite a headache
in its ear-piece.

Elsewhere I doubt
if they had so much trouble. Just
a fluffy moistness
easing in where

the old edges had been. And then
the slow, steady,
drumming, pita-pata
sound, as the rain started.

III   *The Earth*

Well, it was all, really,
a palpable jelly,
touchable, glaucous,
very good to eat

in its own way, if you liked
that sort of thing. I mean before
the day of the cucumbers.
After that, the hard edges

all became round heads,
and there wasn't much
you could do about it.
Not without risking

a hell of a row,
and maybe getting cut,
or swallowed up
in the ice. Let well alone,

I always say.
Take what comes.
You can't win them all. Not
without being one of them yourself.

MARSHALL

It occurred to Marshall
that if he were a vegetable, he'd
be a bean. Not
one of your thin, stringy
green beans, or your

dry, marbly
Burlotti beans. No, he'd be
a broad bean,
a rich, nutritious,
meaningful bean,

alert for advantages,
inquisitive with potatoes,
mixing with every kind
and condition of vegetable,
and a good friend

to meat and lager. Yes, he'd
leap from his huge
rough pod with a loud
popping sound
into the pot : always

in hot water
and out of it with a soft
heart inside
his horny carapace. He'd
carry the whole

world's hunger on
his broad shoulders, green
with best butter
or brown with gravy. And if
some starving Indian saw his

flesh bleeding
when the gas was turned on
or the knife went in
he'd accept the homage and prayers,
and become a god, and die like a man,

which, as things were, wasn't so easy.

IV

VI

FOURTEEN WAYS
OF TOUCHING THE PETER

I

You can push
your thumb
in the
ridge
between his
shoulder-blades
to please him.

II

Starting
at its root,
you can let
his whole
tail
flow
through your hand.

III

Forming
a fist
you can let
him rub
his bone
skull
against it, hard.

47

When he makes
bread,
you can lift
him
by his under-
sides on your
knuckles.

V

In hot
weather
you can itch
the fur
under
his chin. He
likes that.

VI

At night
you can hoist
him
out of his bean-stalk,
sleepily
clutching
paper bags.

VII

Pressing
his head against
your cheek,
you can carry
him
in the dark,
safely.

VIII

In late Autumn
you can find
seeds
adhering
to his fur.
There are
plenty.

IX

You can prise
his jaws
open,
helping
any medicine
he won't
abide, go down.

X

You can touch
his
feet, only
if
he is relaxed.
He
doesn't like it.

XI

You can comb
spare thin
fur
from his coat,
so he won't
get
fur-ball.

49

XII

You can shake
his rigid
chicken-leg leg,
scouring his
hind-quarters
with his Vim
tongue.

XIII

Dumping
hot fish
on his plate, you can
fend
him off,
pushing
and purring.

XIV

You can have
him shrimp
along you,
breathing,
whenever
you want
to compose poems.

AT CRUFT'S

I   *Old English Sheep-dog*

Eyes
drowned in fur:
an affectionate,

rough, cumulus
cloud, licking
wrists and

panting: far
too hot
in your

"profuse" coat
of old wool. You
bundle yourself

about on
four shaggy
pillars

of Northumberland
lime-stone,
gathering sheep.

II   *Weimaraner*

On long
monkey's-paws
like

olive-branches, you
loll, awkwardly
leaning

your dun muzzle against
the veined
oak : your

eyes are what
matter most, those
bottomless, dreaming

yellows, orbed
in
the fine bone

of a German
hunter's-rifle
head.

III *Chow*

With ears
of a Teddy bear : your
tail

over-curled
as if attempting
to open

yourself
like a tin
of pilchards : your tongue

seal-blue : you
roll
in a cuddly

world
of
muscular

bunches, bouncy as
Chinese
India-rubber.

IV   *Shih Tzu*

Top-knot
in a safety-
pin, this

grand-master,
flexible
as a rug, flops,

inclines
his grave head,
is a blur

to the Japanese
photographer,
some foreign

bitch, is he
thinking,
as he wraps

his fleece
in imaginary
sleeves.

V   *Chinese Crested*

Raw
as a skinned
chicken, the

goat's plume
on your brow
ruffled, you

swing a
furred
switch

in the ring
behind you,
fastidiously

tripping
more like a gazelle
than a dog

as you move:
Manchurian,
shivering.

VI   *Schnautzer*

In that
severe
square hook

of a head, he
holds outlines
of his own

dour
elegance to be
scissored

in air: braced
legs
erect

his arched
eyebrows: in grey
mournful

exactitude, his
jaw swivels and:
schnapps!

VII   *Bulldog*

With a face
as crumpled
as crushed

paper, he
shoulders
grumpily

over the sawdust:
someone pats
his

rear, he is
sure,
nevertheless, there

is still
a war on. Everything
everywhere,

pace Leibnitz,
is for
the worst.

VIII   *Dobermann*

Always
on the attack, the lips
drawn

hard back, the
minute
immaculate

teeth, bared
in a snarl, no
love

lost, is
there, then,
between us, or

wasted; in
smooth black
and orange

killing-skin
you sit,
spring-coiled.

IX   *Shetland Sheep-dog*

Am I being
so thoroughly
powdered

to win
a prize, or
just

to please
this ingenious
powderer

in her
pink anorak, you
seem to ask,

with your bright
ice-chips
ripping

the prejudice from
your over-
fluffy ruff.

X   *Pyrenean Mountain Hound*

As if
absorbing the whole
heat of snow

into his noble
coat, he
lifts,

heavy-lidded, the
sombre
gaze

of a glacier-
liver,
knowing

not only how
to revive
the frozen

with brandy, but
what
being wanted means.

XI   *Newfoundland*

Is
a black
solid-bodied

one this, with
a look
of lying

beside a
banked fire,
stretched

in his log-
cabin, his nose
twitching

to the sound
of owls or
coyotes, or even

coal
dropping
in the grate.

XII   *Clumber Spaniel*

If ears
are for hearing
with,

she seems to
waste
acres of expensive

velvet, her
brindled
flaps relaxing

in
friendly
fingers, although,

quite definitely,
closed : at any rate, she
goes

on
dozing
without saying a word.

XIII   *Great Dane*

To be so
big
you could

easily
over-leap my
six feet with your

coat of
many
colours, fawn,

black, harlequin,
is,
after all,

remarkable
enough, so
why whip

my legs
to a jelly
with your tail ?

59

XIV   *Boston Terrier*

Neat
enough for
a tea-party

in that flat
alpaca coat, you
maintain, though, something of

a lawyer's look,
my mid-Victorian,
Yankee

dandy, round-
supercilious-
eyed, fresh

from the courts
after quartering
someone, perched

on your four
ebony
sticks.

XV   *Samoyed*

As if
presenting the
spun glitter of

a new
steel wool: or an
ice tasting

of glacier-
mint: this
polar bundle of

huggable
whiteness, clear
hair

emerging
like tufts
of grown

glass from her
deep skin,
glows.

XVI   *Alsatian*

And yet
without exactly the
appearance of

being violent,
that heavy
tail, tucked

under the firm
hind-quarters,
occasions

doubts about the
advisability
of treating

this law-dog
as if
he was really only

a sheep
in wolf's-
clothing.

XVII   *Irish Setter*

Touch the flowing
thorough-bred
insouciance

of the Old
Ascendancy : the
superior-tweed

mahogany
fur, glossy
as if wet

from the best kind
of trout-stream
recently,

ruffles, furrows
a little
over

the interrogating,
courteous arrogance
of the eyes.

XVIII   *Boxer*

On a strong
rope,
aggressive,

restrained, you
tug
at your corner,

eager
for the bell, and
to be in,

dancing
round the ring,
belligerent in

your
gloved skin,
muscled

as if to
let fists
emerge, clenched.

V

V

PAVAN FOR AN UNBORN INFANTA

AN-AN CHI-CHI
AN-AN CHI-CHI

CHI-CHI AN-AN
CHI-CHI AN-AN

CHI-AN

CHI-AN CHI-AN CHI-AN CHI-AN CHI
AN-CHI AN-CHI AN-CHI AN

CHI-AN CHI-AN CHI-AN CHI-AN CHI
AN-CHI AN-CHI AN-CHI AN

CHI-AN

AN-CHI AN-CHI AN-CHI AN
AN-CHI AN-CHI AN-CHI AN

CHI-CHI

AN-AN CHI-CHI
AN-AN CHI-CHI

CHI-CHI AN-AN
CHI-CHI AN-AN

AN-AN

AN-AN AN-AN AN-AN AN-AN

CHI-CHI CHI-CHI CHI-CHI
CHI-CHI CHI-CHI CHI-CHI

CHI-CHI

67

AN-AN AN-AN
AN-AN AN-AN

AN-AN AN-AN
AN-AN AN-AN

AN-AN

CHI-CHI CHI-CHI
CHI-CHI CHI-CHI

CHI-CHI CHI-CHI
CHI-CHI CHI-CHI

CHI-CHI

TWO EXPERIMENTS

I

Vowel Analysis of "Babylonian Poem"
    from the German of Friederike Mayröcker

"U EE-EI A I AE-IIE-EIE UE EOE U EI; E
EI AAAU (A U EI? OE EEUE E I O EE
    O EIE AUE (EE);
EUE E; AOAIE EI)
EUIOEA; AU EIE AUEAAE IE EE-O (EI . . .)

EO AUE: OE IE A . . ."EEE A E UE
    EI E-O; EI A; A UE . . ."
U AUEUE A; EI U A;
O-E/AU UE
EUE IEE A IEEE UE
AAI I E OOE E I

OI O UA: AUI IF AEIE: U ALE E; OE O;
UIL EA U EE EIEAE; UE EAUE AE;
    A; EI-A-AU . . ."

AU/EIE E OI I A AE UEAIE A
IAUE A-II;
EIE OIE A I EE (IU A E AE; UE
    EIE AAEE OEEI I EEOIE EIE)
A-OIE; I OEE EIE; OAE EI EUEU;
EA IE AE—AUA; AAEI; AAEI (EO
    OE-U U-I-AAE . . .)

UAUIE AO!
UAE; IE OE-/OIEE EA-A-A! EO
    O-EIE . . . (A EIE EIEI I E EIE U?)

IAIIEE EI-IEE
AI AIAIEE AE; UE; AA; EE
... EI AUO UE EIE-E
AUOE..."OI E A..."/A-OI OU' E E...U A-A!
EIE EAE OE-A;
A-AU-E
AAE AIA (IE
 AOE U AOIE: OAUE; OAI; AO)

O-EI-O: OO-I-OU!

EA A AEI/

 (IAUUAIO E OE EEI)

II

Numerical Analysis of "Brazilian Poem"
 from the German of Friederike Mayröcker

  ("..2 2 6 2 3 5: 2 3 3–6 3 8; 3
   6 9 4 8 8; 3 6 10;
   9 3 5; 2–2: 5 4 6!
   2 10 6 6 (8) – 4 3 6 11;
   5 6; 8 7; 2 3 6..")

    9 5 3 5: 2 3 2
   10 4
 5 8; 3 9 2 3; 5 3 4 3 3 9 9: (4!)
 3 6 3 3 4 – 9 6; 7
 3 3 5; 8; 3 3 6; 10 (3 3 7 4 2 3!)

 9 4 3 5 6: 6 3 10:
    5 3 5 7..

4–5 4 9–6 3 5 3 8;
4 7 2 5 6 4 : 7 3 3 8
       3 11 5
9 10 (7 2 6) 7 5 3 6–5 :
(8 5) – 4 2 6 4 : 10 5!
3 3 6 9 6
           (5 4 4)
             (5 4 5)

7 2 5;
3 11 3 4–5

6 4 3 15 4 (6 5)

! 2 6! 3 2 3 6 10 6;
! 2 6!
(10 5 5 4; 10 5 4 5)

2 6 –

        (2 1 7 2 3?)
9

```
D,  LL    L,
LD  NN   ,
ND    L  LLL  ,
D    M  LL        ,
NN  M    D  N  L,
M  ,    M  D :
      LD    M  N  .


MN,    N  N  L,
LD  NN      L,
ML  M  D .
LL  N,    ND    MD ,
L  LL        ,
M  ,    M  D :
      LD    M  N  .


L,
NL  LL  D,
N  LL  M        ,
N    DD  N ,  ND  ,
D    LD  LN  .
M  ,    M  D :
      LD    M  N  .


N    N  ,
M  D  N      ,
D  M  N        ,
LL  LD          .
M ,  M ,    LL  D  .
M  ,    M  D :
      LD    M  N  .
```

NN,
D N:
L N,
N
N   N L.
M ,   M D:
    LD   M N .

D ,
LM DN:
N   ,
L   ,
MN   N   .
M ,   M D:
    LD   M N .

IN ESKIMONO

After Tennyson's The Splendour Falls

Mon iskomones nimon ik sonesk inomo
   Ski mosno esnimes imo ni kosne :
Mik eski onomo nimoki skemon esk osomo,
   Ino esk enimo skimosko mokon ik mosne
Kono, nomon, siko, kis oko meni nimeski sminon,
Inos, mesko ; esomes, miskon, konem, ikiko, mikon.

I nomo, e siki ! Nom ekno kis enomo
   Kes oksomon, imonoki, nimekso konos !
E sonim kos eso mosi nimek ino komo,
   Nom eskes ki sonikso monokim inoksos !
Kono, sek ok inom esk nimono konis mineskon :
Sini koson ; omonok inisko, nesma, skino, mekon.

E kono, smok emo ki nok sino oki,
   Skis onomo ni mosk en ikone mo kosko
Isk osomik eson koms okom ik noki
   Sen osin oni skik eso mon osko
Mesk, esimo, kims, eko sok emon sikone monese
Nos kosemo, nokoki skinom ineki minek omese.

VI

IV

THE HORSEMEN

Budapest, November 4th 1956

There, where the women bent above the grain
In blackened scarves, the stone road broke and veered
Across the fields, towards the flames. No sound
Except the steady grinding whirr of wheels
Woke the slow larks. The sun rose. And its blaze

Across the white plain where the Autumn crop
Stirred in the wind, seared the still-burning walls
Far-off, in dark still. Here, gloved hands lay cold
Along steel hatches where each hinge of oil
Shone in the light rising. That light falling,

Miles on and later, brought the winter night
To boys who lay with petrol and pierced cans,
Awake in cellars, waiting. Some had burned
Only for their idea of what it was
To have been born there, blazed in hatching fire

Along the backs of steel tins, broached and curled
In sticky flame. And now their cold heirs came
West to the bridges and the shallow hill
Below the castle, aged in foreign steel
For a new rising. Somewhere the gold star

Fell in the East and, thinking they were sold
In Africa, they came to level grain
Along this road. And, as their long clear eyes
Veered in the grey light, the steel hatches closed,
And once more they were horsemen, galloping.

AGAINST THE SUN

Malta 1565/1940

I

      So they laid oars
Along the sea, as if in blessing. To
The airs of lashes, and their alms, they moved
In scent of sweat.
     I see them strike and fail,
Recovering, strike and fail.
      On sterns of teak
Where harsh drops rake their awnings, two preside
In silk, inviolate. To the pull of oars
Along the bare thwarts, altering the world,
They crush the grape.
      The sun goes down the sea
Plating their East with blood. And still they row,
Wounding the wave.
      White in their hospital
The cold bread served on silver to the sick
Shines in the light. I see the long bells pitch
Over the islands, and the pious kneel,
Praying.
     Under their awnings here they kneel,
Doing some service.
      The long whips lick at them
With tongues of night. Wine soaked in Christian bread
Absolves their lips. If any spit or die
Their bodies marry salt. In all that sweat,
In order, and rebellion, sick in soul,
The slaves are power.
      So the galleys move
Into what wind there is.

II

I hear their wings
Freshening over Corsica. The guns
Along the grey ships arch and waver. To
The scream of air soon lead will fall like rain
And pit the stone.
                    I see their clean grey eyes
Behind the wings, mounting in honour. One
Lifts a gloved hand.
                    The screws turn. Black as crows
Against the sun, they mount the beaten sky,
Drilling the clouds with fire to clear the sea
And lead their ships.
                    With paired wings, three remain
Holding the gold walls.
                    Empire was all for them
Whom these oppose. Unclassed by age or skin
Their duty moves in eye and ear. All dive
As one in slow flight.
                    Now, below crossed arms
I see the skeleton of one stripped bare
And made a show. No stones, no shells remain
Richer in bare defiance.

III

And so in brine
They sank the bridge of chains.
                    From fort to fort
The brass links bore their chill defiance to
The fire of Asia.
                    This shall rise, and rust,
Only when every flag I see in the East
Rots in our Sacristy, he swore, and crossed
The bare steel in his groin.
                    Under the waves
It dredged and fell, blocking the harbour. There,
Locked up in calm, the Christian ships lay, beached
With splayed oars, like split melon.

79

                                                    One
With gouged pits down its hull had weathered fire
In quelling Tunis. One had lain in Rhodes
Gored by the shells. There, blood of Turkey lurked
Under the hatches, gobbling to be clear
And rise in crescent fury.
                                    Shrink their feed,
He said, *and screw them from the sun.*
                                                    I give
This isle a cross, another said. *Its flame*
Withstood a night of wings.
                                        Against their heart
All pluck and wear it, hearing in the sun
The wings descending, once again the wings
Descending.

                                    IV

                        There, where the lightning struck
And ranged all day, the cold star still remained,
Fish on the stone.
                                Salt licked their lips, the sea
Sprayed them with shells.
                                    If any still believed
His oar might cross the stiff bay, he was bone
Crossed in the water when he sailed.
                                                At their posts
Men drank and burned, staunching their wounds with
    brine
And sterile cloths. Where surgeons lived, they came
With cautery and metal.
                                    If the surgeons died,
They pitched their bodies in the trench. Unburied,
The rotten flesh swelled, burning in the sun
Against their pummelled clay.
                                        And wind,
Lifting hot silks, connived with death. Disease,
Essence of slow death, spiralled.

                    80

V

On the floor of the nave
Where knights in coloured stone lay in their arms
Two dropped a body. There it was dark, and stale
As lard with burnt out wax.

An old woman paused,
Lighting a candle, to look up.

*It was
His nephew,* one said, and ran back.

Between
The flags, beyond the coil of guns,
Hands parted, he was penned in tactics. *He
Is dead, he died well,* someone said.

He came
In marred steel, breathless. As he crossed himself
Beside the dead skin, she held up her flame
Over the face.

One effigy of war
In wax and blood, with rough hands gripped in grief,
Stuck in his mind from Rhodes. A man could paint
The Baptist with his hacked head off, and miss
A mother in the shade.

He touched her hand,
Sour in the groin with dead seed. *For your pains,*
He said, and gave her gold.

Outside, the war
Beat on the stained glass. Here, her candle stirred
Above a lost boy.

As he rose, and knelt
Towards the altar, she reached out, and kissed
His hand.

Unheeding, he walked back, scarring
The bared arms in the aisles.

To war and plans,
Immune from pity, it was honour breached
As cold air in the dry lungs dying meant
For all his line, he moved in action.

81

                              All
The river of his nephew stilled in stone
Sank over plots to future prayers.
                        He
Was building shells, fresh bastions.
                              She knelt,
Honouring Victory.

VI

                  So when it came
The streets were filled with horses. Men walked down
The Kingsway with their hats off. Women, decked
In flagrant roses, watched from windows.
                                    There were fights
Between friends, foreign daggers worn
As open trophies.
                        After that blazing air
The silence was the strange thing.
                              No-one knew
Who was dead, who had lived.
                              Everyone moved
In the calm dream of honour. There were stones
To be laid back on stones, bodies to bury,
Hopes to be fulfilled.
                        And, after all
That holocaust of starved withdrawal, wounds
Licked and re-opened, ordinary grief
At private scores.
                        Watching the last few gulls
Grey in the dockyard, hearing bald-headed men
Telling the stories, I return again
To the Armoury.
                        Here the heroic wars
Blaze in their oiled shields.
                                    Here the impregnable dream
Halts on the islands in its final haze.

NOTES

Despite appearances to the contrary, much of the material in these poems is autobiographical. Quite often a real landscape is described from memory, as in the poems about Malta, Finland and Hungary. Sometimes real people appear under glamorous disguises, as in *Driving West*, where the two "knights" are the author's friends. In the poems about Egypt, Marshall and the giant pandas, real feelings are expressed. Elsewhere there is some invention, as in the plot of *The Soft World Sequence*.

I

DRIVING WEST: A man is driving West to a family funeral haunted by the memory of a woman who is both wife and mother to him. In the dying evening light he lapses into a myth of himself as the sacrificial king of a doomed and blood-sick city. He imagines two versions of his own and the woman's death which connect and overlap in his dream of a nuclear catastrophe. In the first death the woman is entirely obliterated, together with his house and all his belongings. In the second, she is killed in a train accident in a tunnel, on her way, like him, to a family funeral. He imagines that she dreams she has escaped from the train and reached the funeral alive: then she imagines that he has found her dying, still in the tunnel, and made love to her for the last, or perhaps the first, time: finally he imagines a vision of himself as a dying child building a tomb for her beside the sea.

IN THE NORTH: The time is Midsummer, in Finland.

THE MOON-BIRD: The epigraph is from Ouida's eighth novel, *Folle-Farine*, published in 1871.

II

AN EGYPTIAN SEQUENCE: *The Jar*. An adolescent boy is attracted to an older Arab woman. She gives him a box from her dressing-table and he identifies this with an Egyptian canopic jar for containing the entrails of the dead. He begins to imagine himself as a priest involved in a ceremony to raise a mummified Egyptian queen from her tomb, and at the end of the poem the queen materialises as a lioness.

The Lioness. The boy is drinking in an underground room with the woman. He imagines her as the incarnation of the Egyptian queen, the lioness, conceived as a goddess embracing the whole natural world of beasts and plants, and mourning the decline and decay of everything that lives and dies. He identifies his inability to draw closer to her with her phantasmic existence only as a briefly reincarnated ghost. At the end of the poem, he recognises the distinction between the real woman and the imaginary goddess, but at the same time he identifies them in their remoteness from his world.

The House. The boy is alone. He imagines the woman as the Egyptian queen in her lifetime, worshipping the sun, and rising and dressing to meet him in the morning. He identifies her lover with the sun, and conceives the temple of the deity as the house he has built for her as the expression of their mutual love.

THE DEATH-BELL: A young man compares the flight of his mistress to another country with the funeral of an Egyptian queen. He considers the barren outcome of their love.

III

A RIDDLE: The answer is: a piece of soap. Ponge has written a long poem about soap.

THE SOFT WORLD SEQUENCE: The image in the second section of this poem was suggested by a story of Thomas M. Disch's called *Echo Round His Bones.*

IV

The two poems in this section are written in word numbers. Each stanza, or poem, consists of a fixed number of words, though the number of letters and syllables in these may vary. Thus, in *Fourteen Ways of Touching the Peter*, there are fourteen sections each consisting of fourteen words, and each section contains seven lines. In *At Cruft's* there are eighteen poems each consisting of thirty-six words, and each poem contains eighteen lines. So far as I know, this development of writing in syllabics has not been used before in English poetry.

V

The sound-poems, and found sound-poems, in this section should be read aloud to yield their effect: the printed words are offered as a score rather than a text.

TWO EXPERIMENTS: In the numerical analysis, the figures refer to the number of letters in each word of the original The poem may be performed by beating time with any part of the human body — e.g. by clapping, stamping, etc. As in the vowel analysis, the tempo should be as fast as possible without recourse to mechanical aids. The German originals of these poems are in *Tod Durch Musen* (Rowohlt, 1966).

LDMN ANALYSIS OF THOMAS NASHE'S *SONG*: The original is the famous song from *Summer's Last Will and Testament* ("Adieu, farewell earths blisse") and I have used the Elizabethan spelling. The gaps represent the number of space units between each L, D, M or N. The poem should be spoken gravely and slowly in accordance with the mood, feeling and sense of the original.

IN ESKIMONO: The invented language in which this poem is composed is derived from the basic word "eskimono", a portmanteau-form of "eskimo" and "kimono". The poem should be read as a tribute to the strange music of Finnish, a language like an igloo in a

Japanese garden. Each word in the poem contains the same number of letters as its English original. The stanza length and rhyme scheme is also preserved.

VI

AGAINST THE SUN : This poem is based on incidents in the two sieges of Malta, the Turkish one in 1565 and the Axis one in 1940.